Ink Spot
1992
Daniel
Pelavin

DYNAMIC
BLACK
&
ILLUSTRATION

One Hundred Years of Line Art
1900 ≈ 2000

BY LESLIE CABARGA

ISBN 0-88108-113-2 cloth
ISBN 0-88108-114-0 paper
LCC# 93-0713-43

Cover and
Book design,
by Leslie Cabarga

Text set in Cabarga Straight Light,
and Straight Medium.
Title set in Cabarga KOBALT.

Special thanks to
William Ternay for
the use of many
illustrations from
his collection.

Demonstration of
line art reproduction
techniques by
Clarence P.
Hornung
1939

ART DIRECTION BOOKS

10 EAST 39TH STREET, NEW YORK, NEW YORK 10016

Pen outline

Litho Crayon

Contents

Linoleum Print

Spatter

ODE TO AN INKWELL

When a monochrome Dorothy opened her eyes to the blazing technicolor of Munchkin land in the 1939 classic film, *The Wizard Of Oz*, the dawn of the age of color was at hand. Color in movies, and magazines was still a novelty then, used sparingly as budgets allowed. Today, with color almost the rule rather than the exception, the impact of black ink on white paper seems to impress us anew. When printed this combination makes as strong a visual impact as can be achieved.

Black and white represent the opposite ends of the light spectrum. Accordingly, mystic beliefs, and judgments of good and evil—even the inequitable dichotomy between the rich and poor—are wrapped up in issues of black and white. In this complex world filled with "gray areas" we long for basic truths in black and white.

Except for snow and coal, one finds true black and white only rarely in nature. In a 1935 study of the indigenous tribes of New Guinea, Dr. Margaret Mead described the natives' fascination with a red balloon she had brought. It was the brightest red color they had ever seen. One can imagine a similar thrill people must have felt seeing early printed matter. I once heard a scholar assert that the quality of printing, and the

blackness of ink used in the Gutenberg Bible has not since been equalled. That seems hard to believe but consider that Michelangelo's Pieta has never been surpassed either.

In looking over the contents of this book I am somewhat crestfallen to realize that the quality of some work, not 500 years old but only 50 years old, may never be surpassed by artists of today. In part, this is because the purpose of illustration has changed. Back in the1880s when photo engraving was in its infancy, it was difficult enough to simply reproduce a painting or photograph. Magazine captions such as, "a halftone engraving from the original painting by…" helped explain to readers that the woodcut or halftone engraving was in fact a reproduction or recreation of something else.

British artist Edward Johnston once stated, "nothing is reproduced. Something different is produced." And by this he meant to explain the difference between the artist's original work and the version which appears in print. At least, with a woodcut which was locked up and printed with the type, there was no intermediary cameraman to louse up the exposure. What the woodcut engraver produced was what printed–the fewest steps between an artist and his public. For a nickel

Brush

Scratchboard with multiple stroke tool

the newspaper reader held a genuine, limited edition artist's proof in his hands.

These days pretty pictures alone—art for art's sake—are insufficient as illustration. Illustrators still amaze, amuse, and add decorative enhancement to the printed page but now we must bring "concept" to the job. We no longer simply "illustrate," or portray in pictures what is elsewhere said in words. As designer/illustrator Dugald Stermer put it, "When I gave out assignments [as art director of *Ramparts* magazine] I was always looking for the illustrator to make a parallel statement to the article."

In films, television, comics, commercials, and advertisements, the graphic, literal, and verbal elements have become inseparably entwined. The illustrator's accelerated function as a communicator leads her or him to the same goal of succinct expression that the writer strives for. Among our new skills, including computer literacy, basic drawing seems least important.

Despite an attempt to be unbiased in my selection of illustrators there is one area in which I admit to imposing personal taste. All of the illustration in this book is well drawn (and I hope that includes my stuff). There's not a clinker in the batch! I've already suggested that the illustrator of today is 1 part artist and 2 parts communicator. In the current context great drawing almost seems unnecessary. We are not required to faithfully reproduce life in our art as artists were up until the invention of photography. But still I believe the best illustrators, no matter how simplified or stylized their work, have enough knowledge of the human figure, of proportions, and of light and shade, that their work is at least credible or comprehensible. At the opposite extreme are artists like Norman Lindsay, and Heinrich Kley, to name but two, who go the opposite extreme with draftsmanship so exquisite that we are thrilled at their ability to evoke life, and drama, and tension merely through the medium of marks on paper.

Attempting to package the ultimate collection of black and white, line art illustration has been somewhat disappointing. There is simply so much good work out there it would require many volumes to do justice to the subject. Some current illustrators will be annoyed at having been overlooked but many who were asked to contribute failed to. I believe the final contents covers most of the important line art techniques. I regret that there is not more computer illustration in this book (which was produced in its entirety on Macintosh computer). The importance of the computer in graphic arts has become inestimable. And we are only at the beginning of this revolution.

In illustration, as in life, everything is not black and white–not even black and white illustration. Categorizing the work in this book according to production method was frequently difficult. I have placed each piece where it seemed most appropriate but it was often difficult to decide in which chapter to place a brush painting on scratchboard, with pen stipple.

You have before you, I believe, the best collection of black and white illustration to be published within the last forty years, representing most of the major illustrators working in line over the last one hundred years. I hope that it will give added stimulus to the current interest in line art and provide examples to inspire future progress.   –L.C.

Silhouette

Stipple

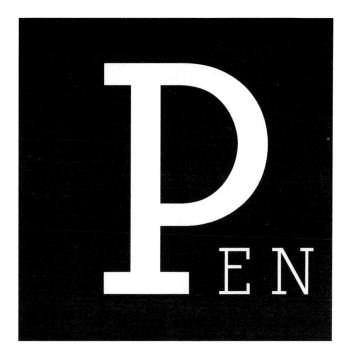

PEN

By volume of work produced, the pen would seem to be the most popular tool for inking. A pen is easier to wield than a brush for at least the pen point rests upon the paper where the brush must hover like a flying saucer. The more limited latitude of the pen stroke also makes it easier to control than the brush. And compared to a woodcut or scratchboard drawing there is less resistance, less labor involved, and no chips to sweep.

In centuries past the pen was used for making plans and sketches but not for finished work. Until photoengraving came into wide usage in the 1880s, pen work could not be directly reproduced. The artist would ink his work on the woodblock and an engraver would then painstakingly cut away the white spaces leaving the drawing intact. By such means the work of illustrators such as Tenniel, Cruikshank, and Nast were brought before the public. Sometimes the engraving improved the original, sometimes not. In any event the published print was only a facsimile of the artist's work. When we look with awe upon

the drawings of Gustav Doré we are actually admiring the skill of his engraver.

Pen technique rose to great heights at the hands of Joseph Pennell, James Montgomery Flagg, and Charles Dana Gibson, whose work, close up, is astonishing for the sensitivity to reproduction.

Whether pen or brush is used, the arm should pivot at the elbow to allow free movement in the wrist and arm. Obviously the rhythmic crosshatching in the work of Heinrich Kley, Edmund Sullivan, and current illustrator Victor Juhasz, could only be accomplished with the greatest confidence, and freedom of movement. In contrast, Franklin Booth managed to create exciting tonal patterns with extremely controlled pen strokes.

For certain artists the stroke of the pen is not a means in itself but a means to an end. The pen "techniques" of Aubrey Beardsley, and Will Bradley, for instance, were almost incidental to the overall design.

In the case of type and lettering, borders, and decorations, the character of the technical pen stroke itself is completely irrelevant except as it defines its subject.

Opposite: **Aubrey Beardsley** The Rape of the Lock, book illustration, 1896

WILL H. BRADLEY

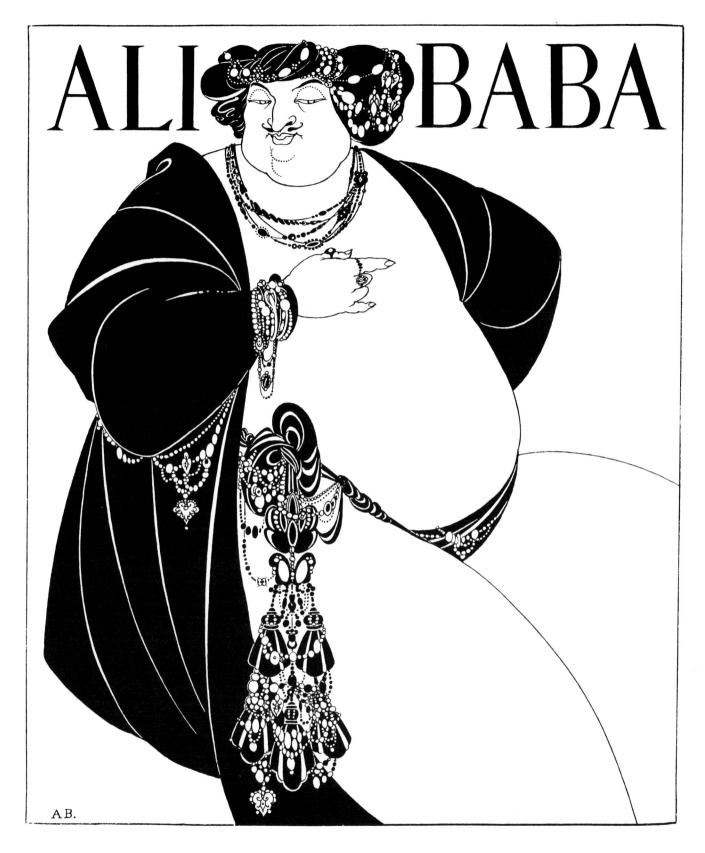

ALI BABA

A.B.

Opposite= The Masquerade,
Will Bradley **1895**

Above= Aubrey Beardsley
{British} 1897

Charles
Dana
Gibson
1901

1898
The Sidewalks
of New York

The term cartoonist applied to Gibson belies the influence of this extremely important artist upon the world of illustration. Seemingly careless for its apparent speed, his inking, like the blown-up dots of a halftone screen, is almost unintelligible up close but coalesces beautifully when reduced (e.g., the woman, below). At left, the chiseled strokes in this woman's face suggest that Gibson likely influenced Franklin Booth.

This is one of a series of drawings by Mr. Flagg, the famous American illustrator. Another will appear next Sunday.

© Ledger Syndicate

JAMES MONTGOMERY FLAGG

James Montgomery **Flagg**
Above=
newspaper cartoon, c. 1935

BERTRAND RUSSELL

Left=
book illustration from **Virgins In Celophane,** 1934

■ *One of America's great illustrators, Flagg built a considerable reputation from pen drawings, paintings, and posters. His "I WANT YOU" remains the most memorable poster of World War I. Flagg's pen style was undoubtedly influenced by Gibson's but stood on its own merit.*

Charles Dana **Gibson** from Life, 1921

People We Can Get Along Without; The couple who hang around for
ten minutes after saying, "good night."

Franklin **Booth** Two illustrations for
Paramount Pictures **c.1925**

One of the most widely imitated illustrators of his time, Booth achieved with pen what
Thomas Bewick had with the woodcut a half-century prior, making mere line serve as a
tonal medium. Booth's crisp technique seemed the modern successor to the woodcut.
His success, in part, lay in the ability to elevate the ignoble advertisement to glory.

Full page advertisement for **Rolls Royce** 1926

Franklin
Booth
Advertisement
for Butterick
Publishers,
1926

Opposite=
Thomas Cleland
Advertisement
for General
Motors, 1924

Cleland was Amer-
ica's leading "fine
arts," graphic arts
designer. According
to Clarence Hornung,
no one could
approach Cleland's
draftsmanship and
imagination.
Influenced by historic
styles of the past,
especially 18th
Century French
design motifs, his
work followed strict,
classic lines. The
example, opposite, is
actually more con-
temporary than his
usual work but it
shows a mastery of
composition, and line.

Pen

Burne
Hogarth
Classroom
demonstration,
1949

■ *Celebrated* Tarzan *car-
toonist Hogarth founded*
The Cartoonists and
Illustrators School *in
New York City which
became* The School of
Visual Arts.

Opposite= **Laurence W. Chavers**
Book illustration from **The Confessions
of an English Opium Eater**, 1932

YOU CAN STILL

by CORNELIUS VANDERBILT, JR.

MAKE A FORTUNE!

The influence of Franklin Booth is seen in the work above, and opposite. Despite the borrowed technique, both artists are extremely competent craftsmen. Their pen strokes, like Booth's, succeed as decoration and still maintain their primary function as a means of shading.

H. R. McBride
Illustration from
Liberty Magazine
1930

Anonymous
Advertising
Illustration
c. 1938

"Cream of" the Crop

LUCKY STRIKE

LUCKY
STRIKE
"IT'S TOASTED"

CIGARETTES

"Lucky Strike quiets
my nerves and does
not affect my voice."

Gertrude Lawrence
Popular Star
of Musical Comedy

Artist
Unknown
for Lucky Strike
1928

The technical perfection, and apparently effortless
execution of these exquisite renderings make it
all the more mysterious that they are unsigned.

"Cream of the Crop"

LUCKY STRIKE "IT'S TOASTED" CIGARETTES

Leo Carrillo,
Popular Stage Star

■ *Although it was not generally the case in 1928, many of today's advertisers prohibit artists from signing their work, fearing perhaps the signature will compete with their message.*

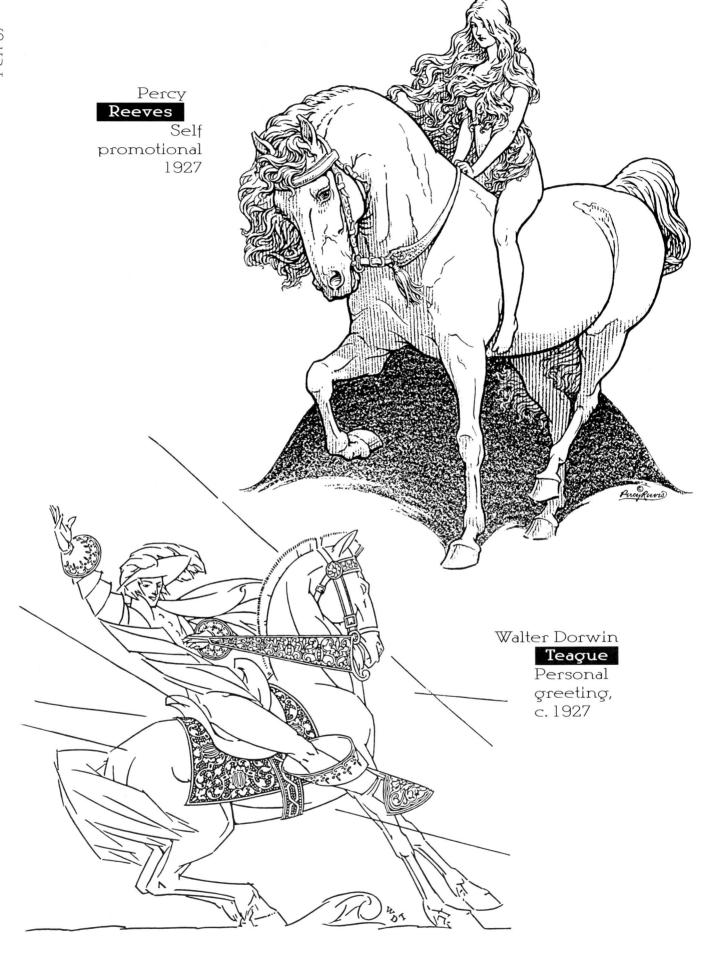

Percy
Reeves
Self
promotional
1927

Walter Dorwin
Teague
Personal
greeting,
c. 1927

QUOD SI DEFICIANT VIRES, AUDACIA CERTE LAUS ERIT

FREDERIC W. GOUDY

Clarence
Pearson
Hornung
1926

Frontispiece—
ATF type
brochure, 1928

Harry Clarke from Poe's **Tales of Mystery and Imagination**, 1933

Left= The Pit and the Pendulum **Above=** Murder in The Rue Morgue

Paul Scheurich {German} 1929
Self promotional advertisement

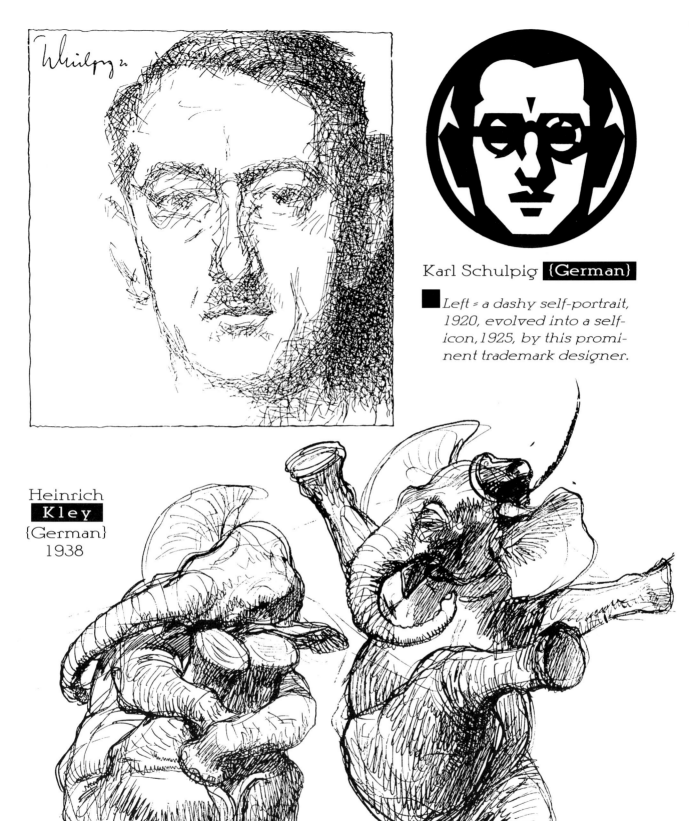

Karl Schulpig {German}

■ *Left = a dashy self-portrait, 1920, evolved into a self-icon, 1925, by this prominent trademark designer.*

Heinrich **Kley** {German} 1938

Betriebsstörung

Die Kampfpause

From
**Sammelalbum
Heinrich Kley**
(Heinrich Kley's
Scrapbook)
1938

■ *Kley could draw anything: man,
woman or beast, (and a few things
God never thought of) all with
astounding anatomical accuracy.
His cavorting pachyderms probably inspired similar scenes in
Disney's Fantasia, released only
two years after Kley's Scrapbook.
Though obviously inked, his facile
pen work is almost indistinguish-
able from pencil sketching*

DRAPERIES

SIAM

CREPE
AND
FAILLE

KLINGER
1925

HYDE BROTHERS FABRICS CORPORATION CLEVELAND

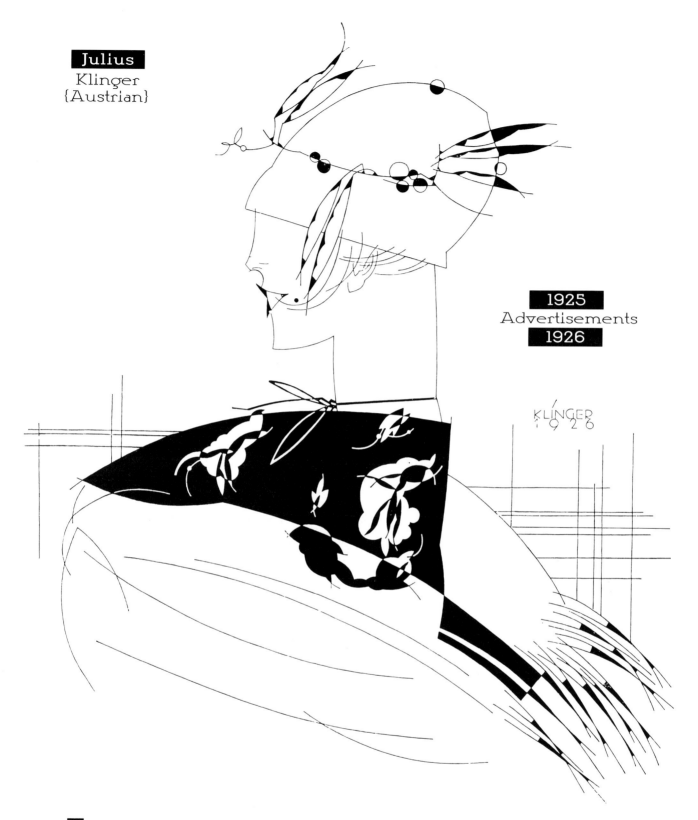

Julius
Klinger
{Austrian}

1925
Advertisements
1926

KLINGER
1926

■ *Klinger was the foremost poster designer of Austria, from the turn of the century well into the 1920s. His work is noted for its sparse compositions punctuated, occasionally by areas of extremely complex, somewhat thorny-looking penwork. We rarely think of delicate pen technique making a poster but many of Klinger's best were done this way, and were printed in black and white. Proving that almost any art looks terrific greatly enlarged.*

BUCHGRAPHIK●

WERBEGRAPHIK●CARL●GADAU

Carl Gadau
{German}
Self promotional
1926

Opposite=
Heinemann
{German}
Advertisement
for a printer
1928

DIE GROSSDRUCKEREI
CARL WERNER
REICHENBACH/VOGTL.

IST DER VORBILDLICH EINGERICH=
TETE GROSSBETRIEB VON HEUTE.
MODERNSTE MASCHINEN UND
ERSTES FACHPERSONAL ERMÖGLI=
CHEN ES, MASSENAUFLAGEN IN
NICHT ZU ÜBERBIETENDER QUALITÄT
SCHNELL UND PREISWERT ZU LIEFERN.

FORDERN SIE DRUCKPROBEN UND VORSCHLÄGE.

Artists
Unknown≈
Primrose
House
perfume,
1931

Lincoln
autos,
1927

Norman **Lindsay** **Above**= Artist
{Australian} Illustrations unknown, {French} for
from **Lysistrata**, **1925** **Renault** Autos, 1932

LITTLE MAN   BIG MAN

Nell **Brinkley**
1935

Brinkley defined the "pretty girl" of the 1920s enveloped in a cloud of curls and endless fabric swirls. Her lavishly colored, extravagantly drawn full-page syndicated comics brought the artist a legion of fans and many imitators. By 1935, above, Brinkley's work, if not her classic cutie, was largely over the hill.

Bernard Boutet de Monvel
for Vogue
1930

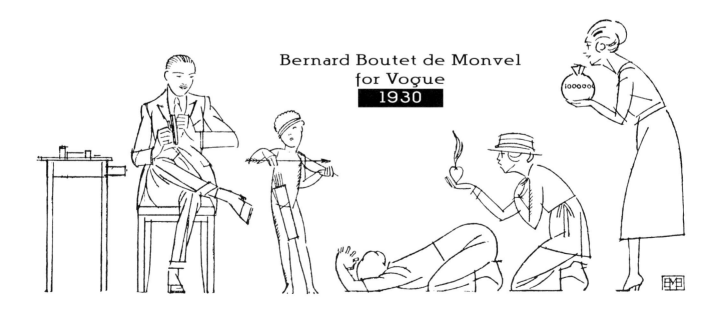

Albert **Dorne**
for Erwin, Wasey & Co.
Advertising, 1939

Diego Rivera
Portrait of the poet,
José D. Frías, 1934

Two expressive pen
drawings by the quintes-
sential commercial artist,
Dorne, and the noted
radical muralist, Rivera.

Boris
Artzybasheff
from his book,
As I See, 1954

Artzybasheff is most identified with outrageous book and magazine illustrations that bordered on the surreal. But he also painted dozens of portraits as covers for Time magazine. Whether in pencil, pen, paint or scratchboard (he often used ⅛" thick celluloid instead of scratchboard), his work was always meticulous in detail and masterful in execution.

ZAP

R. Crumb
Unused
cover design,
1967

■ *The work of R. Crumb is one of the great legacies of the 60s. His very personal ink-ing style, which I call "pen scumbling" grew from an excessive, lifelong habit of sketching in notebooks. His early work inspired a resurgence of interest in nostalgia: old animation, old lettering styles, old music. Crumb brought gritty realism to the comics, desanitizing them in the process. He created the underground comix genre and changed the course of commercial illustration as well.*

Jerry McDonald
Above = 1992
Chicago Gangster
Locations Tours

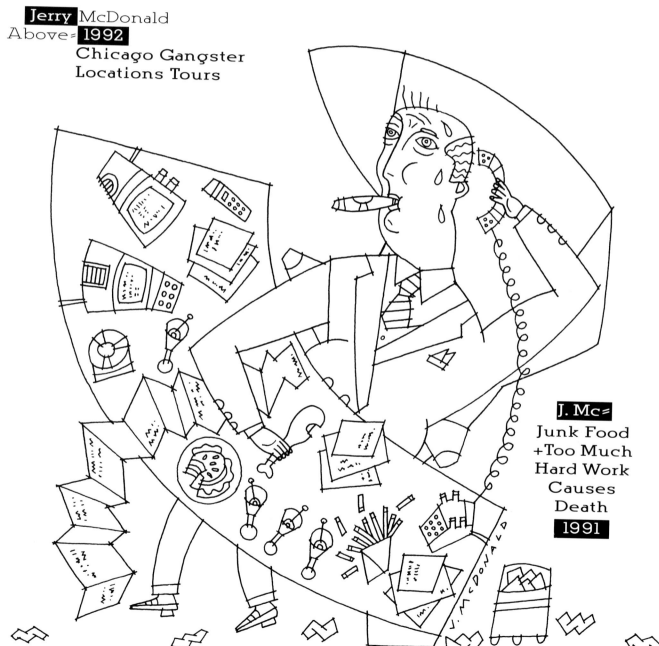

J. Mc=
Junk Food
+Too Much
Hard Work
Causes
Death
1991

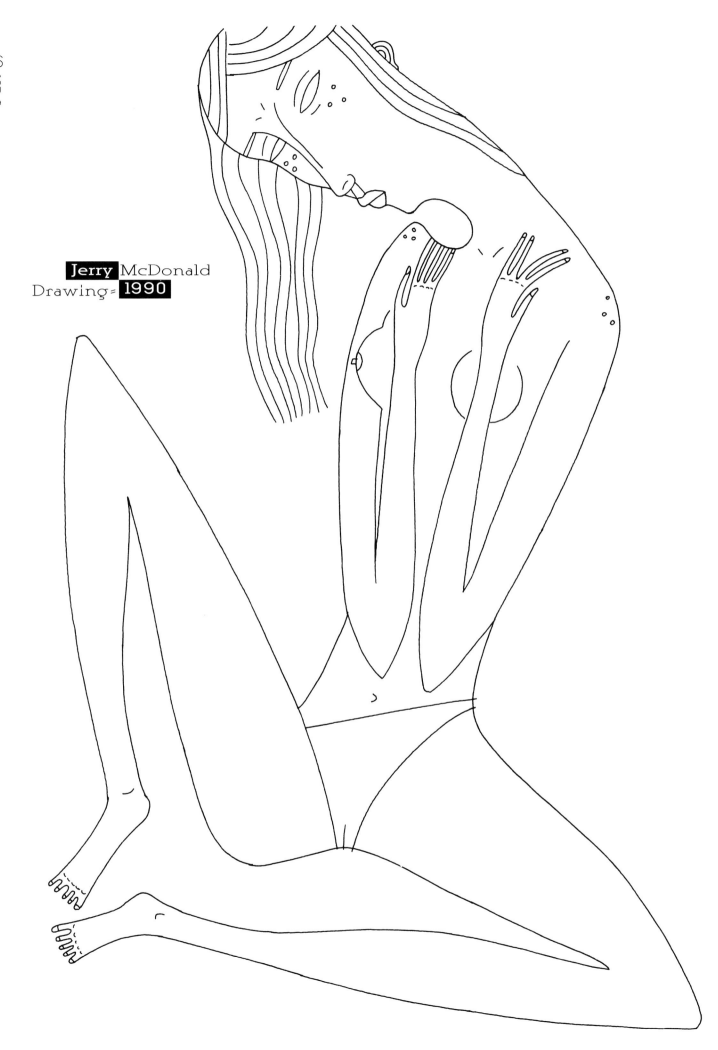

Jerry McDonald
Drawing~ 1990

Jerry McDonald 1990= 53rd and 5th

Ward Schumaker

ZIP THE LIP

Right= Growing
Up a Red Sox
Fan **1988**
Above=
for Simpson
Paper/Pentagram
1991

Ward
Schumaker

Love Poems,
Berkeley
Monthly **1985**

Tim
Lewis
for IBM
Management
Report, 1990

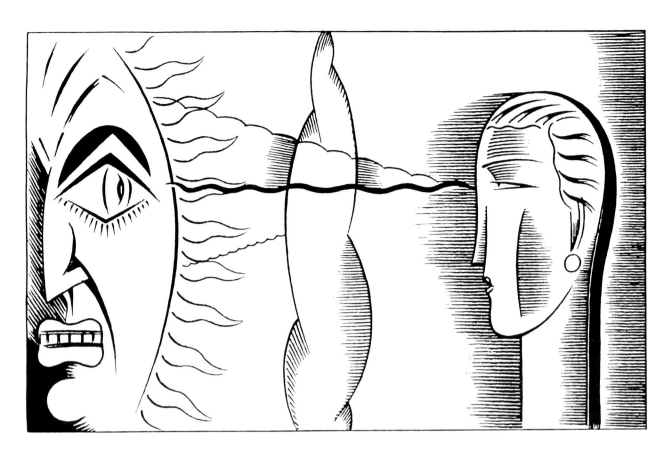

T i m
Lewis
Top= portfolio drawing,
1989
Right= for Financial
Guarantee Insurance
Co., 1992
Opposite page= for
Stanford University
Alumni Magazine,
1991

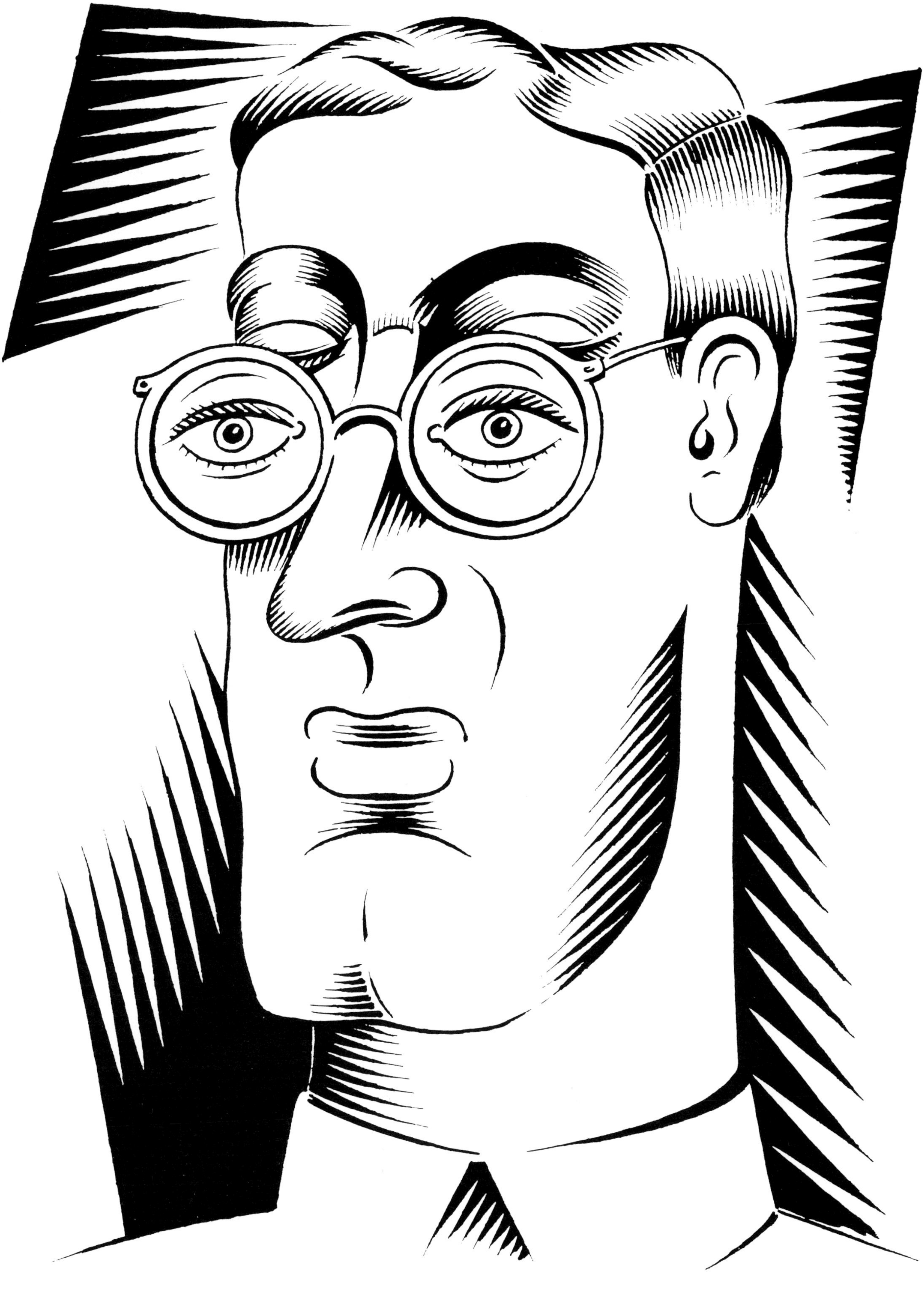

Pen

W.S. Crawford, Ltd. {British} 1928
Left=
Advertisement
for German
Chrysler.
Opposite=
JJ Whiskey

Leslie Cabarga
Unpublished
trademark

Above=
Tim Clark
New West
Magazine
1980

Left=
1930s
Stock
Advertising
illustration

Daniel **Pelavin**
Two spot illustrations= **1992**

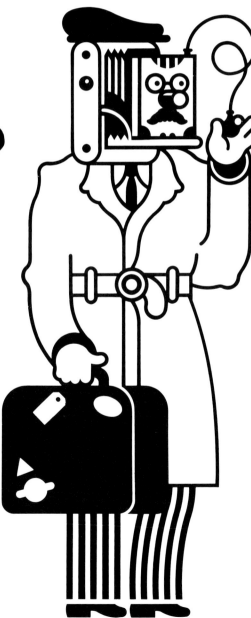

■ *Pelavin has built
an industry around
clever spots as these.
In fact, order his
catalogue and collect
them all!*

Barry Zaid
Advertising illustration for Winter House =
1971

Zaid, and fellow Push Pin alumnus, Seymour Chwast, were among the first
designers to inspire the Art Deco revival which rages on after twenty years.

Illustration for Saturday Night
Magazine, 1985

Jean **Tuttle**
Self-promo-
tional greeting
card, 1985

Below⸗
Illustration for
New York
Times, 1987

To Leslie — Happy Easter!

█ *Tuttle's work advanced the trend
in robust, decorative feathering
which is currently so conspicuous.
Working on scratchboard with
brush and technical pen enables her
to easily make refinements and
corrections. Much of Tuttle's work is
now done on Macintosh computer
(see page 191).*

Art
Spiegelman
1974

■ A master of the "comic noir," Spiegelman's pen technique could be called perfunctory but it serves well the needs of this Pulitzer Prize- winning author of Maus.

Elwood Smith has parlayed his penchant for old comics like Herriman's Krazy Kat, and Segar's Popeye, into a personal style which has made him one of today's most successful humorous illustrators .

Elwood
Smith
1992

P.E.T.
1927

By the 1920s knock-offs of the "bighead" cartoon characters, first popularized by F. G. Cooper in Life the comic weekly, could be found everywhere in advertising. Aside from the novelty factor, an oversized head succeeded in small space advertising where a correctly proportioned figure would be too small to show any facial expression. Bottom example= in the mid-1920s, possibly to avoid over-saturation of ink, a vogue developed for etching white dots into any solid black areas. The effect was pleasing.

Artist
unknown
c. 1935

Charles
Howell
"H"
c. 1924

Gary **Lund** Two illustrations **1992**
Spirit Speaks Magazine

Suter and Lund are two of the best conceptual illustrators in America today.

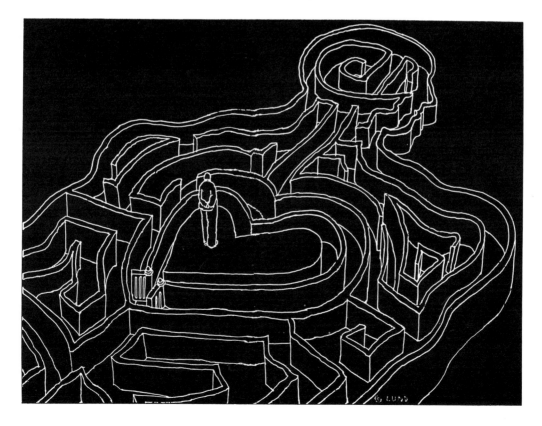

62

Pen

Edmund J. **Sullivan** c. 1920
from The Rubáiyát of Omar Khayyám

The reproductions of Sullivan's work unfortunately leave much to be desired. Perhaps his originals were too fine, his ink too weak for the camera's eye. Or maybe my source, an original book, was just poorly printed. Sullivan made dozens of beautifully drawn and inked illustrations for his Rubaiyat which are among the most incredible book illustrations I've seen.

David
Suter
c. 1980

■ *Suter's illustrations have strong composition, great drawing, and a dramatic sense of light and shade. His habit of introducing visual riddles into his work has made him unique among his peers. His pen work reminds me somewhat of Rockwell Kent, which should be a positive endorsement of it. That Suter is related to Britain's revered poster designer, E. McKnight Kauffer must be no accident.*

Illustrations
for The New
York Times
Book Review

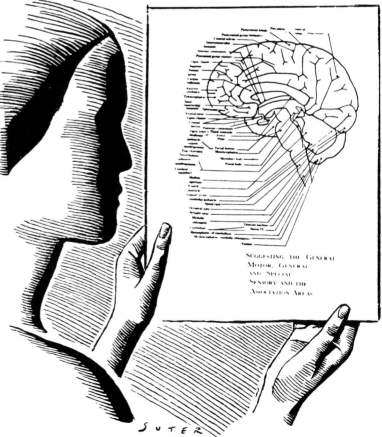

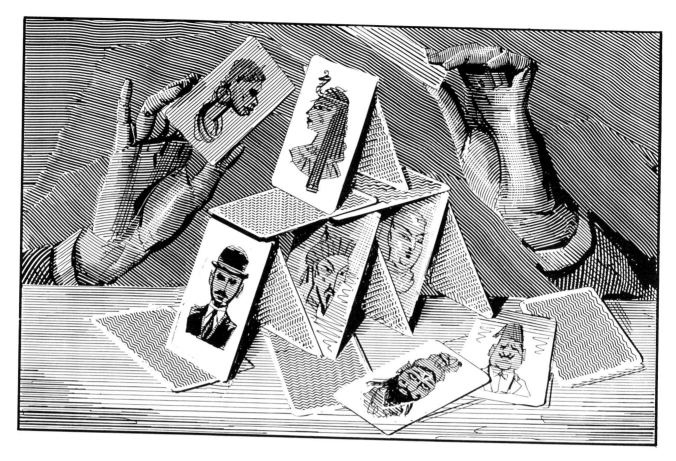

Elliott **Banfield**
Opposite=
House of cards, 1981;
Art, 1988
Right=Lincoln, 1989;
Die and Coins, 1985

■ *Using technical pens and custom made templates, Banfield brings a unique dimension to line art. His phenomenal portrait of Lincoln surpasses the original steel engraving to become a pop art icon.*

Victor
Juhász
Right= Personal
greeting card,
1992 Below= ad
for Merril Lynch,
1990
Opposite=full
page illustration
for
Mother Jones
magazine, 1986

*Almost in self defense
over the steadily
declining quality of
crowquill penpoints,
Juhász occasionally
resorts to a rolling ball
writer (see opposite:
XXX Stand) which
adds zip and spon-
taneity to his already
fluid style.*

SECURITIES
TRANSACTION
**EXCISE
TAX**

Loederer c.1938

Ernest **Hamlin Baker** 1932
Drawn with white ink on black paper

Artist
unknown
for
J. Walter
Thompson
Advertising, 1942

■ *An interesting illustration for its scratchy, textural shading. The even gray tones contrast beautifully against the open, white areas, and solid blacks. The car in the garage and the lettering on the signs indicate that the artist basically can't draw but he makes up for it with strong design. This is a transitional piece which—even to the bad drawing—predicts the coming style of the 1950s.*

Above
for Franklin Union Oil, **1942**

Gene **Deitch**
Comic strip-
Terr'ble
Thompson
1955

From the mid-1940s to the early 1960s a backlash was mounted in reaction to four decades of slick magazine illustration which held such men as Norman Rockwell, and Haddon Sundblom as the ideal. Suddenly, purposely rough and shaky inking, unevenly feathered shading lines (see above), and bad drawing became not only acceptable but fashionable. Illustration had lost its easel painters and academicians but discovered the designer.

Artist
unknown
{British}
for Gee &
Watson
1954

Joe
Feher
for Sealed
Power
Corp.,
1943

BRUSH

A brush stroke is a living line possessed of great warmth and variety. By bearing down on the brush as the stroke is made, a thicker line is produced which gives volume and weight to form.

A brush becomes an extension of the artist's inner vision forming a seamless connection from the brain through the hands to the paper. Even a slapdash, careless brush technique, in the hands of an artist who draws well, can still produce dynamic results. But when brush-strokes are applied in an intentional manner we are awed at the beauty of each line.

As a drawing tool the brush holds several advantages over the pen. Few pen points match a brush's flexibility, its speed and sensuality. The brush is dipped less frequently than a pen and the danger of unexpected splotching is less.

The brush is a chameleon tool easily imitating other mediums such as woodcut/scratchboard, and pen. Rapid strokes with a fairly dry brush produce something like the textured appearance of litho crayon. The adept may even draw straight lines with a brush rather than finishing these with a technical pen as is more common. Brush technique, like handwriting, varies considerably from artist to artist, even those using the same kind of brush.

The brush makes great "speed lines." Shadow areas are inked in quickly. The weight of brush strokes adds drama to a picture which is why it is the preferred inking tool of comic artists.

A brush requires more initial practice than the pen and many are thus afraid of it. When mastered, however, a brush provides greater freedom and versatility.

Opposite: **Herbert Roese** Self promotional advertisment, 1930

Herbert M. Stoops
1924

ARMISTICE NIGHT

FIRES twinkling everywhere in a land that has been dark for more
than four years. You could lift your head without getting a cold sen-
sation in the small of your back—your coffee was hot—corn willie fried
was a brand new dish. The powder from Jerry's fixed ammunition made
a blaze that would kindle wet wood, and the replacements illuminated
the whole sky with German rockets and Véry lights.

"Just like Broadway," says some sentimentalist.

Herbert M.
Stoops 1924

As a trench soldier during World War I, the popular illustrator Herbert Stoops kept a visual diary of the event which was later collected in a portfolio published by The Jello Company. Handling the brush as a sketching tool, Stoops used bold contrasts of light and shade, and vigorous strokes to convey the drama of the moment.

Kenneth McLellan
1922

Artist unknown
c.1935

Herbert M. Stoops
1924

C. B. Falls
Illustration
for the book,
**Vast
Horizons**
c.1947

Adolph Treidler

c.1948

WALT KELLY

The
POGO
STEPMOTHER
GOOSE

Opposite⹃
Walt Kelly
Cover for **The
Pogo Stepmother
Goose**, 1957

Right⹃
C. B. Falls
calendar illus-
tration, **The Tea
Pot**, 1926

Below⹃
**Wallace
Morgan**
men's wear
advertisement,
1924

Rockwell Kent

Rockwell **Kent**
Opposite page, and
above= advertise-
ments for The
Commercial National
Bank & Trust Co. of
New York, **1934**
Bottom, both pages=
illustrations from
Moby Dick, **1930**

Dora
DeVries
for Saks
Fifth
Avenue
1948

Anonymous
Advertising
Illustration

for Pacific Mutual
Life, 1942

C. Peter Helck
for Otis Elevator, 1934

Frank B. Hoffman
for Erwin,
Wasey & Co.,
1924

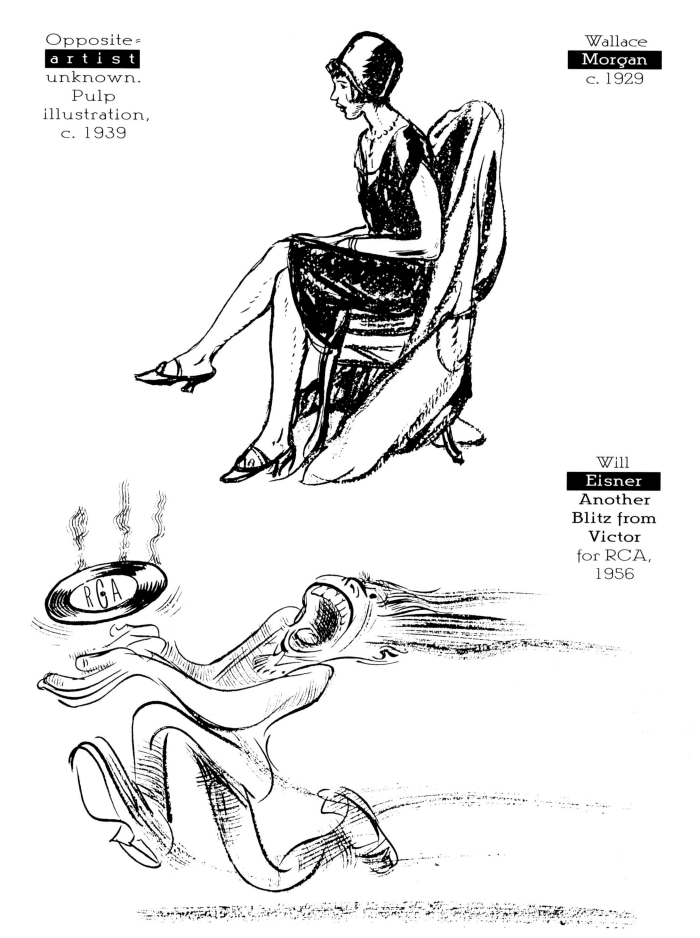

Opposite—
artist
unknown.
Pulp
illustration,
c. 1939

Wallace
Morgan
c. 1929

Will
Eisner
Another
Blitz from
Victor
for RCA,
1956

RGA

Will
Eisner
Advertising illustration
for RCA Victor
1956

■ *Penciling at first loosely, Eisner's final drawing actually emerges in the inking stage. He gained fame in the 1940s with his trend-setting syndicated comic strip,* **The Spirit,** *and is currently risen like the phoenix from the ashes of several inter-vening business ventures to reclaim his place as one of America's finest comic artists. His way of suggesting form and shadow through swelling strokes makes him, in my opinion, one of the best brush inkers of all-time. For a dry-brush effect, he advises, "first flatten the brush point against the paper using the thumb nail."*

Above = F. G. Cooper c.1934
Below = Illustrations for **Tarzan** by Rex Maxon, 1929.

W i l l
Eisner
Splash panel
from **The Spirit**,
1950

Chris
Ishii= **The Piel
Brothers**, animated
characters for
Piel's Beer, **1957**

Bryan **Vollman**
1992

A brush with white paint on black paper
produces an effect resembling a wood cut.

Opposite=
Steve Leialoha
from **The Shadow,** 1992

With the confidence of a
master, comic illustrator Leialoha
guides his brush unerringly
through the most complex
foliage and feathering.

Above=
Holland
for London
and
North Eastern
Railway, 1931
Left=
Neal Bose,
1927

Leslie
Cabarga
Right= illustration for
Time, Inc., 1983
Below= Illustration for
Money Magazine, 1991
Bottom right=
spot illustration for
Premiere Magazine,
1990

■ *Working on frosted mylar,
the author uses white-out
to cut into his brush inking
for a woodcut effect.*

Edward **Penfield**

Calendar Illustrations, 1924

Leslie
Cabarga
1992

F. G. [Fred] **Cooper** c.1942

FRED COOPER

■ *Cooper, who in 1905 promulgated the "big-head" character, went on to inspire several generations of illustrators (including the author, above) with his decorative, virtually calligraphic inking technique.*

draw me!

TRY *for* AN ART SCHOLARSHIP

Artist
unknown
c. 1936

Steve
Leialoha
1992

Linda **Bleck** 1992

Opposite= Full page advertisement for Temik Corp. Above= Illustrations
for **History of Sex**, Impress Publishers.
Below: Christmas greeting card for VanAlt Group.

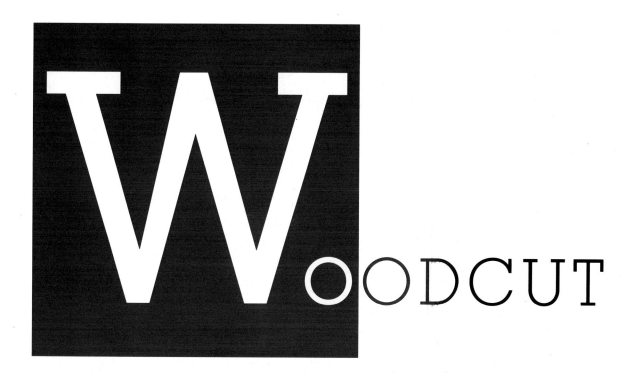

WOODCUT

Of all printing mediums the woodcut has the longest history. Woodblocks were, after all, the first printing plates. And the first truly dynamic graphics were woodcuts produced in the fifteenth and sixteenth centuries consisting of heavy outlines, and bold contrasts of dark and light. Yet the prints of early woodcut artists such as Dürer, and Holbein, though highly detailed, resembled pen drawings rather than woodcuts. Tonal areas were executed more as flat tints rather than modulated shades.

It was left to the English engraver Thomas Bewick in the 1780s to fulfill the woodblock's potential as a tonal medium. Instead of the purely technical work of removing bits of wood inbetween inked lines, Bewick saw the block as black and his strokes as white. The result was a full spectrum of tonal values. Bewick's inspiration made the wood engraver an artist in his own right instead of an interpreter of others' pen drawings.

The celebration of stylistic diversity in the twentieth century, finds woodcuts running the gamut of styles from bold, simple line art (resembling medieval work) to tonal "paintings" of almost unfathomable complexity. The woodcut "look" is so popular that many of today's artists use pen, and brush—even computer—to imitate it.

Possibly it is the physical act of chiseling pictures in a block of natural wood that gives the true woodcut print its strength. From the earliest woodcuts of the Middle Ages to current efforts, the emotional response we feel from looking at a powerful woodcut illustration has not diminished.

A near cousin of the woodcut is the linoleum cut. The surface of a prepared linoleum block is more yielding than the woodblock surface but incapable of holding as fine lines. The strokes are therefore fatter and rounder and for this reason linoleum cut illustrations are usually delightful to look at. The boldness of linoleum cuts, and the ease of hand printing, make them well suited to greeting cards, and small-run poster production. They also make dynamic illustrations.

Opposite= **Aaron Douglas** Defiance, from the Emperor Jones series, 1926

Thomas
Nast

Cartoon for Harper's= **By inflation you will bust**, 1873

■ *Nast is the father of the American political cartoon. His work
appeared regularly in Harpers Weekly throughout the Civil
War, and beyond. With nothing but pen and ink he waged war
against hypocrisy, injustice, and corruption (where is he now
when we need him?). Along the way, he created the definitive
portrayals of Uncle Sam, and Santa Claus. The cartoon above
looks like a pen drawing but closer inspection reveals that it is a
woodcut engraved over Nast's pen sketch. One giveaway is the
miniscule white lines which interupt the crosshatching.*

Opposite= **Engraver**
unknown= advertisement for Scott's Emulsion, 1893

Childhood

Anonymous
Probably steel
engraving=
George Washington

Right=
1874 Wood engraving
from the painting,
Spring, By Pierre A. Cott.

Two stunning examples of the engraver's craft from the turn of the century. The clarity of technique, and perfection of form-following parallel linework make these excellent for study.

Above: Trademark (possibly steel engraving) for Wamsutta Mills, c. 1920s
Below: Advertising Illustration, Bowery Savings Bank by **F** 1922

THE ROYAL TAILORS
CHICAGO — NEW YORK
TRADE MARK REGISTERED

Above=
Trademark for
Royal Tailors
c. 1925
Left=
advertising
illustration for
Kuppenheimer,
1924

*This sparkling,
unsigned wood-
cut faithfully
reproduces
every detail of
J. C. Leyendecker's
original painting
including the
strokes of his
famous brush
technique.*

John Held, Jr.

THE ROAD TO RUIN

John Held, Jr. 1920s

Famed for his pen illustrations which seemed to define the 1920s Flapper era, Held was also an avid wood engraver (as well as a talented sculptor) who produced scores of images like these which lovingly lampooned the sentimentality of the gay nineties. Held's work appeared frequently in the popular humor magazines of his day.

Top,
Kurt
Scheele
{German}
book
illustration,
1934

P. E. Vibert
{French}
N u d e
1930s

Eric **Gill**
{British} Book Illustration=
The Passion **1927**

Above left= Franz Masereel
{German} from
Mein Stunden Buch `1928`

Above=Gemma
P e r o {Italian} 1930s

Below= **Paul Dietrich**
{German} 1938

Hermann Paul {French}
from **La Danse Macabre** 1930s

Charles **Evers** {German}
1936

Fritz Kredel {German} 1933

Hans
Gutgesell
{German}
Book
illustration,
1934

Raphaël
Drouart
{French}
Book illustration,
**La Tentation de
Saint-Antoine,**
1925

C. B. **Falls**
Amateur
Night,
calendar
illustration
for
Marchbanks
Press, 1926

Will
Dwiggins
Calendar
illustration
for
Marchbanks
Press, 1925

The Set-Up

Unsigned illustrations (probably by Steele Savage) from the book,
The Wild Party, by Joseph Moncure March, 1929

The Wild Party

ROYAL MAIL CRUISES
DAILY__PROGRAMME

ROYAL MAIL CRUISES
DAILY__PROGRAMME

= W = I = L = L = I = A = M =

Robert F. **Heinrich** for Edison-Dick Co.

Opposite, top= Advertising illustrations
by **Kenneth D. Shoesmith** {British}
Opposite, left= unsigned portrait of
Theodore Roosevelt. Opposite, right=
birth announcement by **Frank Riley**

woodcut

Robert F. **Heinrich** advertisement, c.1924

Gustav Doré Illustration from The Bible, 1886

Above⸗
Three illustrations from
Pencil Points Magazine, 1929,
by **William S. Rice**
Right⸗ The Waldorf Astoria,
1929, by H. Paulson Legg
Opposite⸗ Unidentified
woodcut by Peck

Rudolph Koch,
book illustration,
c. 1925

Left=
Bertrand Zadig
for George H.
Doran, Co.
1926

Lynd
Ward
Illustrations from
God's Man,
a novel
in woodcuts,
1929

Overleaf=
illustrations from
Frankenstein,
1934

Lynd **Ward**

Joseph
Tiberino
1992

Philadelphia artist Tiberino brings a painter's eye and a poet's heart to his extremely fluid woodcuts.

GOD BLESS AMERICA

Wilfred
Jones
Cover for
Scribner's
magazine,
1927
cut on linoleum

Jeanne
Fisher
Three linoleum
cut illustrations,
1982

Curtiss **Sprague** Linoleum cut, 1928

Norman **Kent** (date unknown)
Portrait of Aubrey Beardsley

Two linoleum cuts: Norman **Kent** (dates unknown)

IMPEACH

NIⱧON

Above=
linoleum cuts by
Nancy Stahl, 1980
and Right=
Leslie Cabarga
for Outside magazine,
1978

Opposite=
Anonymous
Linoleum cut, 1974

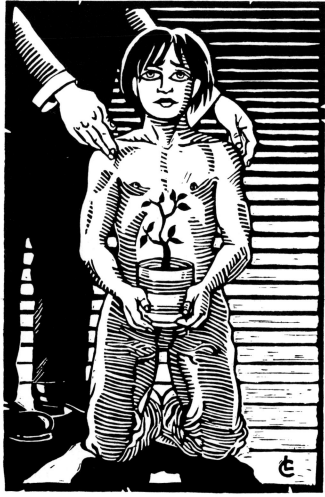

Nancy
Doniger

Top: **America Without
Apartheid**, New York Times,
1986 Above: **Short
Circuiting a Nightmare**,
New York Times, **1992**
Right: **Honeymoon**, for
Ailanthus Poetry Journal,
1986

Nancy
Doniger
for The
New York
Times,
1992

■ *A different kind of "cutting edge technology" is used by Doniger. Her work is prepared with Amberlith, a clear acetate sheet coated with a transparent orange film. The camera "sees" amberlith as black which is why it is usually used for color separation overlays. Placed over a pencil drawing, the areas of the image which are to appear black are cut out with an exacto or swivel knife. "White" areas of the amber film are then pricked up. The cleanest possible lines and corners are achieved in this way. Corrections are a little tricky but at least white-out is avoided.*

Leslie
Cabarga
Amberlith icons for
Money Magazine,
1989

SCRATCH BOARD

Scratchboard is a white, clay coated paper on which ink is painted and then scraped away to reveal white or "light." Pre-inked scratchboards are available but these preclude a selective blacking in where those areas which will remain white are left unpainted (thereby helping the artist to ascertain bearings). Irwin Smith, Boris Artzybasheff, and others recommended using an airbrush to apply ink evenly to the scratchboard surface since an uneven coat of ink can interupt the consistency of a stroke. The working sketch is then applied to the inked surface with white chalk or colored pastel.

Developed in the 1880s, scratchboard was a bi-product of the development of the halftone screen. By scratching white lines through a continuous tone work of art it was intended that those tones would be broken down into minute, individual segments which the camera could "read" as line, much as the halftone screen eventually provided.

The beginner invariably cuts white lines into scratchboard as he would draw an ink line on white paper. This is akin to producing a negative. The proper approach is to view the act of scratching as shedding light upon darkness. The most stunning examples in this chapter are those with bold contrasts of light and dark.

Scratchboard yields results very similar in appearance to a woodcut. In comparing printed examples the two are sometimes difficult to tell apart. As for execution there is no doubt that scratchboard is the easier of the two. For one thing, a woodcut must be printed before it can be viewed in final form. Errors in a woodcut have to be cut out and a new section of wood carefully spliced back in. But scratchboard illustrations may be corrected by re-inking areas that have already been scratched off.

Some artists will work on scratchboard for the ease with which corrections are made, no scratchboard effect, per se, being desired. Tip: frosted mylar has a superior inking surface, from which mistakes may be erased with a special eraser and/or scratched.

Opposite: **Bill Russell** The Southern State, magazine illustration, 1990

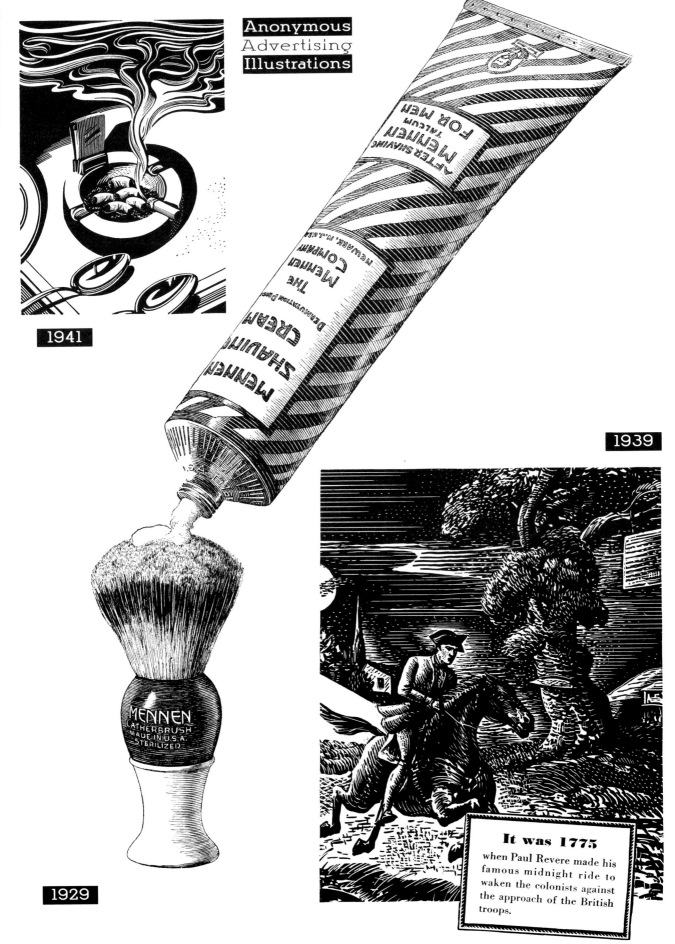

138

Scratchboard

Anonymous
Advertising
Illustrations

1941

1929

1939

It was 1775
when Paul Revere made his
famous midnight ride to
waken the colonists against
the approach of the British
troops.

1928
Hy Rubin

1940

Jac Huffman **1941**

Scratchboard

Walter
C o l e

Advertising illustrations for Shawmut Bank
1 9 4 1

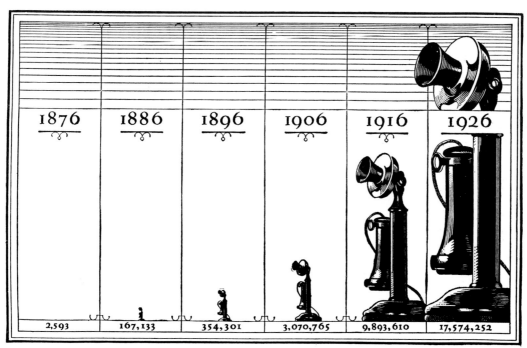

1876	1886	1896	1906	1916	1926
2,593	167,133	354,301	3,070,765	9,893,610	17,574,252

Guido & Lawrence
R O S A

Advertising illustrations for AT&T
1 9 2 6

Anonymous
Advertising
Illustration
1941

Technically adequate, the monotonous range of this illustration fails to create much excitement. But perhaps the intention was to place the focus on the watch.

Irwin Smith

Advertisement
for U. S. Steel
1941

Irwin Smith

Advertisement
for U. S. Steel
1941

Smith's ability to render various tones and textures, not only convincingly but with great bravado of contrast, led him to the top of his field. Note the disciplined parallel strokes used in the hand above compared, opposite, with the more casual, carved effect on the glove and above the upper lip. Works such as these usually begin with excellent-quality photographic reference.

Above = anonymous advertising illustration for Scott Tissue, 1940
Walter **Cole** for Coca Cola, 1941

Walter **Cole** for Coca Cola = **1941**

The Marchbanks Press, New York

114 East 13th St.   *Tompkins Square 6-6420*

Lester Beall
for the Chicago
Tribune
c. 1947

Raymond
Lufkin
for Marchbanks
Press, 1935

Boris Artzbasheff
for Time, Inc., 1934

W. Parke
Johnson
Self promotional
advertisement,
1927

W. PARKE JOHNSON
147 West 23rd Street
Chelsea 4382

W. Parke **Johnson**
Self-promotional ad, 1940

■ *Johnson's dramatic handling of textures, especially his glowing metallic surfaces, makes him, in my opinion, the superstar of scratchboard. What halftone
photograph would dare challenge the power of such renderings?*

W. Parke **Johnson** c. 1948

Bill **Russell** **Losing Face** from Saturday Night Magazine, **1990**

Bill **Russell**

Opposite⁼
**The Port Chicago
Explosion** from San
Francisco Focus, 1992
Magazine

Above⁼ illustration
from Toronto Business
Journal

Alex Murawski Hot Food for Hopper Paper Co., 1991

SILHOUETTE & STIPPLE

The appeal of the silhouette dates back to the first time man saw his own shadow. Despite its lack of detail the silhouette is capable of fantastic expression. Like a shadow it seems to capture the soul of the subject. A silhouetted view is a privileged one implying that we are in a darkened alcove, our image of the subject affected by the glare of outside light to which our eyes are unaccustomed.

Silhouettes, both painted and cut with scissors, became popular in seventeenth and eighteenth century Europe. Especially in Germany where the national aesthetic taste embraced woodcuts and graphics with heavy blacks. "Profilists" found enthusiastic patronage in every principality. Silhouettes remain popular in German graphic arts to this day.

The silhouette artist fullfilled a special need in Colonial America where good portrait painters were scarce. Itinerant profilists provided cheap likenesses until the photograph eliminated the need for their services. Colonial figures and cameos remain popular with latter day American silhouette artists.

Stipple work always looks amazing not only for the vivid tonal contrasts achieved but for the sheer labor involved. Stipple is almost like a manual halftone screen with all the customizing such a process would allow. Few copy-camera technicians know how to punch up the contrast on a photographic halftone to achieve white whites and black blacks as the stippler does. Thus the effects of stipple often approach a sort of hyper realism.

A woman I once met who described herself as an "excessive pointilist" eventually developed carpal tunnel syndrome from stippling. The pulp artist, Virgil Finlay, an avid stippler, used to wipe and re-dip his pen after applying ever dot. Stippling may be an especially compulsive activity to engage in but the results are wonderful to see.

154

T. U. Freyberg {German}
Magazine
advertisement, 1929

E. M. **Enders**
{German} 1937

Richard Rothe
{Austrian}
from the book,
**Das Marlein Vom
Wunderscherlein,**
a paper cut-out
book about paper
cut-outs, 1937

Top=
Curtiss **Sprague**
left, from **The**   right, advertising
Sketch Book, 1929   illustration, 1929

Surrounding=
The Cat Came Back,
from John Martin's
Big Book 1925

Opposite= Fred **A.** Mayer
for the New York Times, 1940

Max
[Maximus]
Schwartz
1939

MAXIMVS

FRED A MAYER

Silhouette

How a Poster Artist Portrays "Movies in the Home"

One of the Daring Creations by Lucian Bernhard Whose Unusual Work Has Made Him Conspicuous in European Art. This Poster Attracted Much Attention at a Recent Exhibition at the Art Centre, New York City. It Depicts in Graphic Art a Typical Family Party Enjoying an Evening of Movies at Home.

Lucian
BERN HARD
{German}
1926

The publicity above was a blessing for the renowned Berlin poster artist, Bernhard who, upon moving to New York City initially found few commissions. Art directors felt his style was too modern for American tastes.

Right=
1929

Above=
Diana **Bryan**
The Marshal
Plan, 1987

Right= **Mary**
Eames
1926

Diana
Bryan
1991

Bryan's exuberant paper cut-outs
have graced the pages of national
magazines for over twenty years.

R.A.
Loederer
art print, c.1920

INTERBOROUGH RAPID TRANS

OUR MEN
KNOW
THEIR JOBS

The Subway Sun

THE SAFEST
RAILROAD
IN THE WORLD

VOL. VIII No. 33   THOMAS E. MURRAY, JR., RECEIVER   1936

FRED COOPER

Fred Cooper
1936

A lady writes us and complains
That men who cross their legs in trains
Soil women's dresses with their shoes—
If they'd desist 'twould be good news!

Norman Lindsay {Australian}
Illustration from the book, **Lysistrata**, 1925

164

Stipple

☞ Dieses Inserat fehlt in der Rubrik:

Wer macht Entwürfe

Industriegraphiker

E. H. Jeschke

Seehof bei Teltow
Uhlandstraße 11
Tel. Berlin 73 84 26

G. H. Jeschke
{German}
1929

W. P. Schoonmaker
1940
for National Surety
Corporation

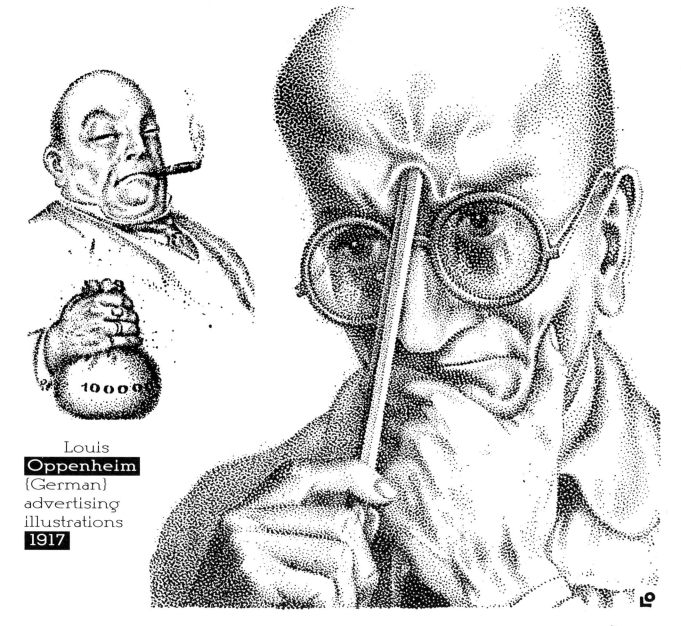

Louis
Oppenheim
{German}
advertising
illustrations
1917

W. R. **Crawford**
Dash stippling
(dappling?) for
Rbt. Burns
Tobacco, 1916

Helen Sewell Illustration from the book, **The First Bible**, c.1947

Roy G. **Krenkel** Personal work showing
influence of Norman Lindsay, c. 1950

Virgil Finlay
Pulp illustration, 1951=
As Others See Us

Jon **Whitcomb**
c.1935

■ *Better known for his painterly magazine illus-
trations throughout the 1940s and 1950s, Jon Whitcomb's advertising illustration is
as notable for its striking composition as its exquisite stipple technique.*

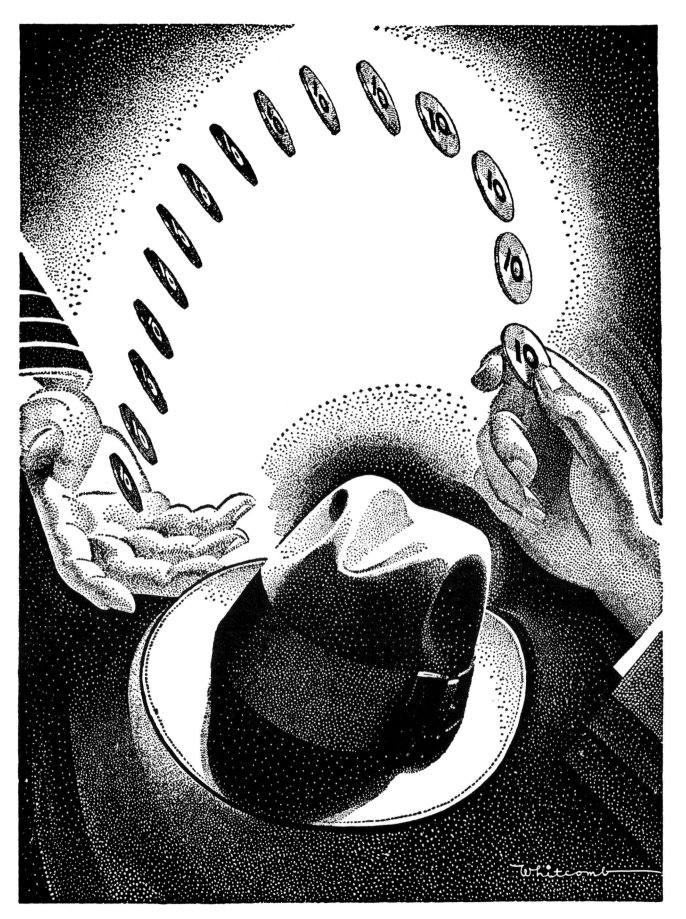

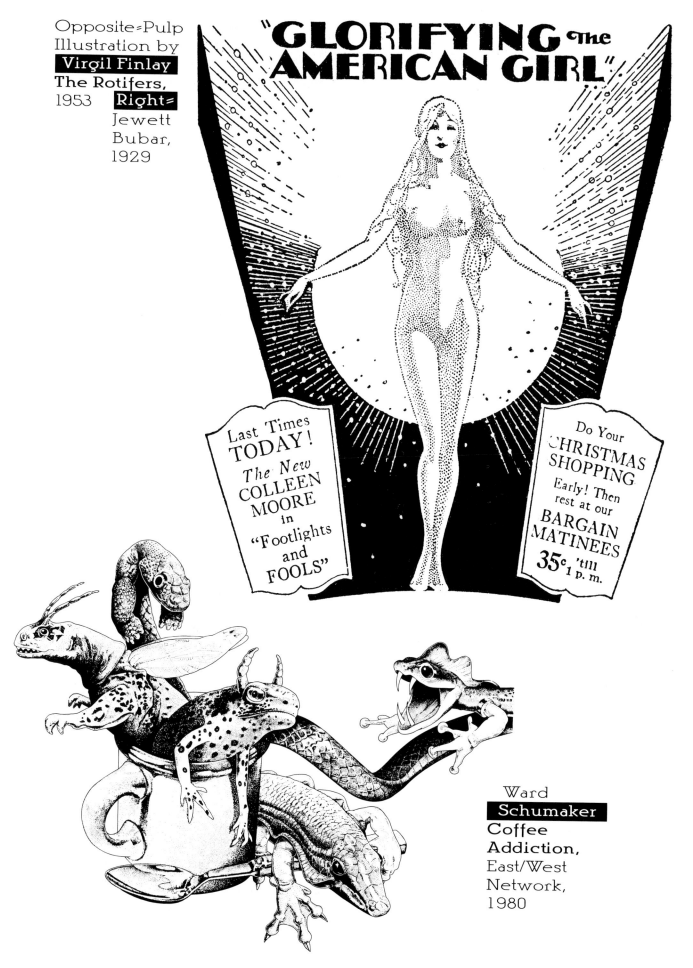

Opposite=Pulp
Illustration by
Virgil Finlay
The Rotifers,
1953   **Right=**
Jewett
Bubar,
1929

"GLORIFYING the
AMERICAN GIRL"

Last Times
TODAY!
The New
COLLEEN
MOORE
in
"Footlights
and
FOOLS"

Do Your
CHRISTMAS
SHOPPING
Early! Then
rest at our
BARGAIN
MATINEES
35c 'till
1 p. m.

Ward
Schumaker
**Coffee
Addiction,**
East/West
Network,
1980

Alex **Murawski**

Two illustrations for
Master Typographers=
Marvin, and
Topsy Turvy,
1992

Alex **Murawski**

Etc.
LITHO CRAYON,
SPATTER, & COMPUTER

Since artwork in any medium may be photographed in line this chapter could be a large one. Of the more popular line reproduction media covered in this book only crayon and spatter remain to be discussed. Oh, and and let us not forget, the computer!

A litho crayon gliding over a rough paper surface produces a broken, inconsistent line which is essentially a halftone. Crayon was used on stone lithography plates at the turn of the century for this very purpose. A black Prismacolor pencil on cold-press illustration board will achieve a similar effect and will print well. Once, artists boards in a variety of textured surfaces, just for line art reproduction, were commonly available. They are now rare but may still be found.

Spatter work is done by dipping an old toothbrush in ink then riffling the bristles toward you to make the ink spatter upon the paper. This takes some experimentation as to how much ink should be on the brush, how far the brush should be from the paper, and how to get the spatter in the right spot. Generally masks are used—prepared frisket or simply cut paper—to protect both the non-spattered portions of the drawing (and the spatterer). Spatter is useful for producing gray, halftone effects with interesting, uneven speckle patterns.

Every student who learns computer graphics immediately gains the equivalent of a lifetime of technical inking skills. Actually, the computer obviates inking since whatever is "drawn" is thus "inked" in an unlimited variety of strokes and fills. Gone are the days of clogged Rapidographs, imperfectly cut french curves, blotchy ink compasses and the cursed whiteout. As long as we stick with geometrically-based graphics the computer is our ally (accounting for the current popularity of such work) but for drawing fluid curves or swelling strokes a pen or brush is not yet dispensable.

Opposite: **Edmund J. Sullivan** from **The Rubáiyát of Omar Khayyám**, c.1920

Litho Crayon

P. A. L. 1896

Jan
Klausing
Movie advertisement,
1929

Albert
Stermer
Cover illustration for
Colliers magazine,
1906

F. Front
{French}
Cartoon
for Frou
Frou
magazine,
1901

— Maman !... Regarde le beau clair de lune !
— Tu sais bien que j'ai la vue basse !... Tu montreras ça au vicomte.

Denys Wortman
from the syndicated
comic, **Mrs. Rumpel's
Rooming House,**
c.1929

*Deft
strokes of a litho
crayon conjure a
moving scene
of New York
City tenement
life.*

Jules **Cheret**
{French} 1896

■ A rough, litho crayon sketch
by this renowned poster artist, has been
rendered upon the stone by the
chromist, Bergon.

Litho Crayon

Herbert
Roese
Full page,
self
promotional
advertisement,
1927

■ *Less is more—much more—
in this elegant and dramatic
illustration. Excellent
drawing holds the piece
together, and realistic
underlighting gives us a
sense of being there.*

"ON WITH THE *SHOW*"

Litho Crayon

Artist
Unknown
Full page
advertisement
for the film,
**On With the
Show,**
1929

Roy G.
Krenkel
Pencil sketch
from his book,
**Cities and
Scenes from the
Ancient World,**
1974

Litho Crayon

NANCY STAHL

Nancy
Stahl
Illustration
for The New
York Times,
1978
Opposite:
artist unknown
circulation
advertisement
for The New
York Times,
1936

■ *Forty years sepa-
rate these two New
York Times illustra-
tions yet the tech-
nique remains the
same: black-leaded
pencil on textured
board permits line
reproduction of
tones without use of
a halftone screen.*

Artist unknown
Newspaper
advertisement,
c. 1928

■ *A combination
of drybrush and
crayon resulted in
an illustration well
suited to reproduc-
tion on newsprint.*

1929 {German} artist unknown

Carl Marr {German; München} book cover, c.1928

Bertrand Zadig 1928

Opposite:
anonymous
newspaper adver-
tisement, c. 1928

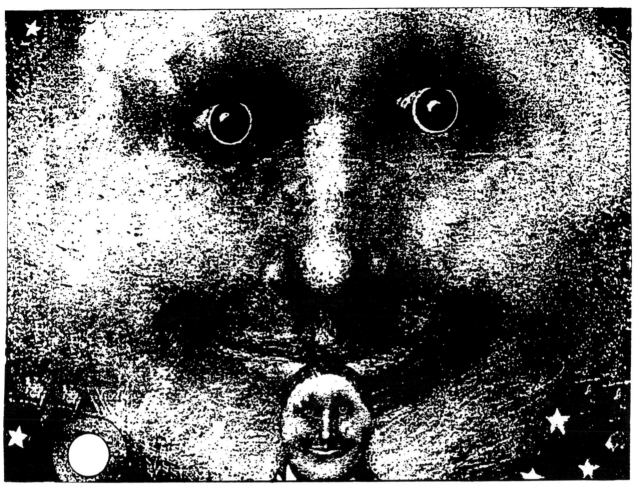

Gary Lund 1991

■ *Ink, spattered on acetate with a toothbrush, then judiciously scraped with an exacto knife, provides former animator Lund with the unique effect, above.*

James
Billmyer
Advertising
illustration,
c. 1928

Gary
Lund
for Spirit Speaks
magazine,
1993

JAMES BILLMYER

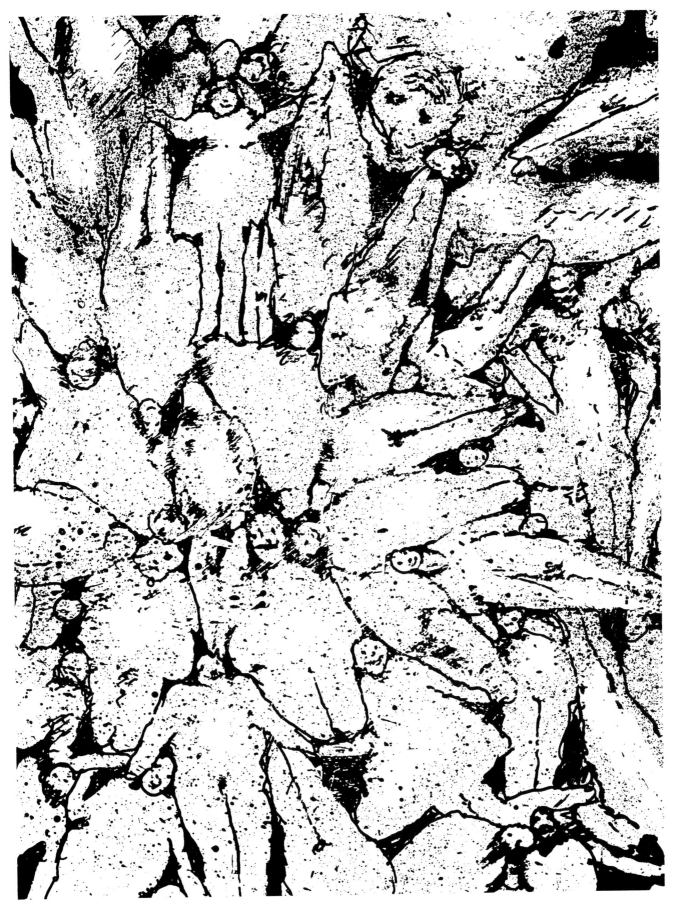

The great Hirshfeld! His illustrations for theatre, film, and dance reviews have delighted newspaper readers for decades. Hirshfeld's caricatures are always uncannily accurate, and his pen technique consistently beautiful. No random cross-hatching in Hirshfeld's work. The placement of every line seems carefully calculated by this master designer. There is something different and wonderful to be found in every job by Hirshfeld.

Al
Hirshfeld
Newspaper illus-
tration, pre-*Nina*,
in pen and ink
with spatter
c. 1938

'Remember the Day'

Javier
Romero
1992

Private Eye
Downhill Skier

Javier Romero

Above=
**Business
Meeting**
Right=
Moving

1992